THE NBA PLAYOFFS

IN PURSUIT OF BASKETBALL GLORY

MATT DOEDEN

MILLBROOK PRESS · MINNEAPOLIS

Copyright © 2019 by Lerner Publishing Group, Inc.

All rights reserved. International copyright secured. No part of this book may be reproduced, stored in a retrieval system, or transmitted in any form or by any means—electronic, mechanical, photocopying, recording, or otherwise—without the prior written permission of Lerner Publishing Group, Inc., except for the inclusion of brief quotations in an acknowledged review.

Millbrook Press
A division of Lerner Publishing Group, Inc.
241 First Avenue North
Minneapolis, MN 55401 USA

For reading level and more information, look up this title at www.lernerbooks.com.

Main body text set in Adobe Garamond Pro Regular 14/19.
Typeface provided by Adobe Systems.

Library of Congress Cataloging-in-Publication Data

The Cataloging-in-Publication Data for *The NBA Playoffs: In Pursuit of Basketball Glory* is on file at the Library of Congress.
ISBN 978-1-5415-4153-5 (lib. bdg.)
ISBN 978-1-5415-4382-9 (eb pdf)

LC record available at https://lccn.loc.gov/2018022630

Manufactured in the United States of America
1-45312-38807-9/10/2018

CONTENTS

INTRODUCTION: WHERE LEGENDS ARE MADE   5

1 SUPERSTAR SHOWCASE:
THE HISTORY OF THE NBA PLAYOFFS   7

2 FROM HANNUM TO KING JAMES:
THE GREATEST GAMES OF THE NBA PLAYOFFS   19

3 FROM LEGENDS TO LAYUPS:
MEMORABLE MOMENTS OF THE NBA PLAYOFFS   40

4 LOOKING AHEAD:
THE FUTURE OF THE NBA PLAYOFFS   56

SOURCE NOTES   60

GLOSSARY   61

FURTHER READING   62

INDEX   63

INTRODUCTION:
WHERE LEGENDS ARE MADE

The roar of the crowd fills the arena. The clock is ticking down, and everything is on the line. A player fakes a shot and darts toward the hoop. He rises, floating the ball over the outstretched fingers of the defense. The ball hangs in the air, bounces off the backboard, and rolls around the rim. It's the National Basketball Association (NBA) playoffs, and the season rides on this shot.

In the NBA, stars are born in the regular season. But it's the playoffs where legends are made. The games get more physical. The pressure ramps up, and the stakes are at their highest. For more than 60 years, the NBA playoffs have been the peak of professional basketball. Every team is chasing the same goal: the NBA championship. Only one will achieve it.

Kevin Durant won the 2018 NBA Finals Most Valuable Player award after scoring 28.7 points and grabbing 10.7 rebounds per game in the championship series.

The Chicago Stags played in the Basketball Association of America from 1946 to 1949.

1 SUPERSTAR SHOWCASE:
THE HISTORY OF THE NBA PLAYOFFS

When the Philadelphia Warriors and the Chicago Stags met in the 1947 Basketball Association of America (BAA) Finals, the series came with little fanfare. While the popularity of college basketball had exploded in the previous decade, the professional game was struggling to attract the public.

Philadelphia held a 3–1 series lead and would become the BAA champion if they could win Game 5. Warriors forward Joe Fulks was the star of the series so far. The productive shooter had led the league in scoring that season, and he dominated in the Finals as well. Yet as the final moments ticked away, Fulks didn't steal the show, but Philly guard Howie Dallmar did.

Dallmar was an unlikely hero. At his best, he was a smooth-passing guard with little scoring ability. But Dallmar wasn't at his best. Pain in his feet hobbled him, and he hadn't been expected to play, much less be the hero.

Philadelphia coach Eddie Gottlieb kept Dallmar on the bench to rest his aching feet. But as the game came down to the final minutes, the guard talked his way onto the court. "He sat there, pestering me to let him in," Gottlieb said. "When it came down to that point where I thought we might win the game, I sent him in."

The game clock ticked under a minute with the score tied 80–80. The Warriors had the ball. Everyone expected Fulks, who had scored 34 points in the game, to take the shot. Yet Dallmar found an opening in the defense and rose up for a jump shot. The ball bounced on the hoop and then fell through for Dallmar's only points of the game. Moments later, the Warriors were celebrating an 83–80 victory and the first BAA championship.

Howie Dallmar played three seasons in the BAA, all with the Philadelphia Warriors.

More than 70 years later, the BAA is a distant memory. The Chicago Stags have faded into history, and the Warriors moved to California to become the Golden State Warriors. Yet the BAA's first championship series was the foundation of the biggest spectacle in professional basketball—the NBA playoffs.

THE BEGINNINGS OF THE NBA: FROM MINNEAPOLIS TO LOS ANGELES

In the late 1940s, two rival pro basketball leagues battled to win the hearts of basketball fans. The National Basketball League (NBL) had been around for about

10 years, compared to just a few seasons for the BAA. The NBL had a longer history, but the BAA was slowly winning the battle for fans. Besides Chicago and a few other big cities, the NBL had teams in smaller cities such as Sheboygan, Wisconsin, and Toledo, Ohio, where teams often played in small gyms. BAA teams mostly played in bigger cities with bigger gyms, and the league had an aggressive plan to move into more major markets.

As the BAA grew in popularity, it became clear which league was likely to win the battle for fans. In 1948 four NBL franchises left the league to join the BAA. Most notable among them were the Minneapolis Lakers, which featured the best player on the planet, center George Mikan. Mikan led the Lakers to the BAA championship the next season, despite breaking his hand in the series.

From the moment the Lakers left, the NBL was doomed. So in 1949, the leagues agreed to merge into a new league, the National Basketball Association (NBA). The NBA continued to recognize BAA statistics and championships beginning with the 1946–1947 season. The new-and-improved league of 17 teams split into three divisions, with the top four

George Mikan puts up a shot for the Minneapolis Lakers. He stood nearly 7 feet (2.1 m) tall at a time when most players were much shorter.

teams in each division advancing to the playoffs. While the division structure may have made sense for the regular season, it left the league with a messy tournament bracket in 1950. After the division finals, three teams were left standing—the Lakers, the Syracuse Nationals, and the Anderson (IN) Packers. Syracuse had the league's best record, so the Lakers and the Packers faced off in an extra series. The Lakers won with ease, setting up the first true NBA Finals.

Syracuse, led by 21-year-old big man Dolph Schayes, was no match for the Lakers. Minneapolis was loaded with talent, and they had a home-court advantage unlike any other. Their home arena, the Minneapolis Auditorium, couldn't accommodate a standard-size basketball court—it was several feet narrower than usual. The Lakers, who were used to the narrow court, thrived in front of the hometown fans. In the series-deciding Game 6, played in Minneapolis, Mikan was unstoppable. The biggest star in basketball scored 40 points, and the Minneapolis fans celebrated the team's first official NBA title. The Lakers dynasty was on.

EVOLUTION AND DYNASTIES

In the 1950–1951 season, the NBA trimmed down to two divisions, the Eastern Division and the Western Division, for a tidier playoff bracket. Meanwhile, the league eliminated many of its franchises in smaller cities. By 1953 it had shrunk to just nine teams.

While change was inevitable in the new league, one thing stayed the same. The Lakers dominated in the playoffs. Minneapolis won four of the first five NBA titles. However, the team fell into decline after Mikan retired in the mid-1950s.

The league was primed for a new dynasty. So when the underdog Lakers shocked the Western Division in 1959 to advance to the Finals, it was only fitting that they faced the up-and-coming Boston Celtics. The young Celtics dominated the Lakers to win the title. The series marked the beginning of a new era in the NBA as the

Bill Russell takes a shot for the Boston Celtics against the St. Louis Hawks during the 1960 NBA Finals.

Celtics went on to build a dynasty for the ages. A year later, the Lakers packed up, left Minneapolis, and relocated to Los Angeles, bringing the NBA to the West Coast. Minneapolis wouldn't have an NBA team for three decades.

Dynasties were nothing new in professional sports. But fans were discovering that in the NBA, they were the rule rather than the exception. More than in any other sport, one outstanding player could instantly vault a team into the league's elite. When a team had the best player in the league, it was a fair bet they'd win a lot of games.

THE BLACK FIVES

The NBA formed at a pivotal time in the history of the United States. The civil rights movement, the struggle for equal legal rights for black Americans in the 1950s and 1960s, was gaining steam. The NBA officially integrated in 1950, allowing black players to step onto the court with white players. Before that, blacks were not allowed in the NBL and the BAA. Many of the game's top black players played for barnstorming teams—called Black Fives—that traveled the country. The New York Rens (right) were one of the most successful Black Fives teams before disbanding in 1949.

Black Fives games were spectacles. Basketball was the main course, and music and dance helped draw crowds. While no official playoff determined a champion, sportswriters informally honored one team each year as Colored Basketball's World Champion. The Black Fives faded out after the NBA integrated in 1950.

For the Celtics, that player was center Bill Russell. Russell wasn't the flashiest superstar in the league. But when crunch time came, nobody was more certain to deliver. From 1957 to 1969, the Celtics won 11 NBA titles, including a stunning eight in a row from 1959 to 1966. In 1968 and 1969, the Celtics won championships with Russell serving as both a player and the team's head coach.

THE GROWING LEAGUE: FROM THE ABA TO PLAYOFF EXPANSION

The NBA quickly became big business. Beginning in the 1960s, the league started adding teams. Meanwhile, as the popularity of pro basketball grew, others looked to get a piece of the action. In 1967 the American Basketball Association (ABA) formed and hired George Mikan as its first commissioner.

The ABA knew that it faced an uphill battle to compete with the NBA. So it marketed itself as a more exciting, wide-open brand of basketball. It introduced several rule changes to increase both scoring and the pace of play. Most notable among them was the three-point line—a revolution in the game. The Pittsburgh Pipers, led by future Hall of Famer Connie Hawkins, defeated the New Orleans Buccaneers, four games to three, to claim the league's first championship.

For nearly a decade, the competing leagues battled for the best players and the most loyal fans. The ABA's fast-paced, flashy style caught on quickly. But it lacked a major television deal and wasn't able to make as much money as the NBA did.

Still, the ABA held on long enough and grabbed just enough of the basketball-watching public's attention to force the hand of NBA owners. In 1976 the leagues agreed to merge. Four ABA teams, the Denver Nuggets, Indiana Pacers, New York Nets, and San Antonio Spurs, joined the NBA. The remaining ABA teams disbanded after their owners received cash buyouts.

The NBA, meanwhile, had continued to grow. In 1971 the league expanded

San Antonio Spurs forward Larry Kenon soars for a basket in the late 1970s. The Spurs have won five NBA championships, more than any other former ABA team.

to 17 teams split into two conferences, each with two divisions. By the 1976–1977 season, the number of teams had increased to 22. The popularity of playoff games made them the league's biggest moneymakers, so the playoff format expanded right along with the league. Starting in 1975, 10 teams—five from each conference—qualified for the playoffs. The four lowest-seeded teams in each conference kicked off the first round with lightning-quick three-game series. The new format ramped up the excitement for fans and helped generate extra revenue for owners. But many coaches and players disliked the change, calling the short series too unpredictable. In such a short series, they argued, it was too easy for the lesser team to beat a better one.

FROM SUPERSTARS TO SUPERTEAMS

By the 1980s, the NBA was bigger than ever. A stream of star players fueled the league's growth. In the early 1980s, Larry Bird and the Celtics battled Magic Johnson and the Lakers as the league's two most storied franchises renewed their rivalry. Between them, they dominated the league. In the decade, the Lakers won four titles and the Celtics claimed three. The clashing dynasties ignited an increased interest in the sport, and the league was quick to capitalize on the growing success. Starting in 1984, the NBA playoffs expanded to its current field of 16 teams—eight from each conference.

In the 1990s, Michael Jordan and the Chicago Bulls took the game to new heights. In the 2000s, it was Shaquille O'Neal, Kobe Bryant, and the Lakers again. Dynasty gave way to dynasty, and the fans ate it up.

Shaquille O'Neal was a nearly unstoppable force in the NBA. He averaged more than 23 points per game over 19 seasons.

THE WNBA

In the 1990s, the popularity of women's basketball was on the rise, fueled by interest in the women's college game, as well as international and Olympic play. In 1996 NBA owners started the Women's National Basketball Association (WNBA) to showcase the talents of the game's greatest female players.

Like the NBA, the WNBA has been a league of dynasties built around star players. The Houston Comets, led by Cynthia Cooper, won the WNBA Finals in each of the league's first four years (1997–2000). In the 2000s, the Los Angeles Sparks, Detroit Shock, and Phoenix Mercury ruled the league. And in the 2010s, Maya Moore (*right*) and the Minnesota Lynx were the league's elite team.

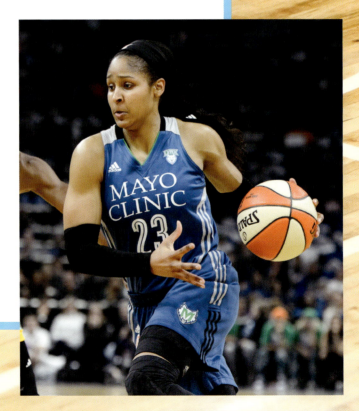

WNBA CHAMPIONSHIPS

4 Minnesota Lynx
4 Houston Comets
3 Phoenix Mercury
3 Los Angeles Sparks
3 Detroit Shock

Dwyane Wade and LeBron James helped the Heat win back-to-back championships in 2012 and 2013.

A new NBA era dawned in June 2010. Forward LeBron James, widely regarded as the game's best player, left the Cleveland Cavaliers. It wasn't the first time a big-name free agent had switched teams, but it marked a change in the way teams are constructed, with the power shifting from NBA front offices to the players. James, along with fellow All-Stars Dwyane Wade and Chris Bosh, engineered a series of deals to play together on the Miami Heat. It was, in many ways, the birth of the superteam.

The idea that the NBA should have a somewhat even distribution of talent was over. Suddenly, star players built their own superteams, leaving a top-heavy league filled with a few great teams, some mediocre teams, and a lot of teams that had little hope of competing.

Superteams brought out plenty of critics. Some said that leaving too many teams and their fans without hope was bad for the game—even if television ratings were soaring. The critics were loudest in 2016 when star forward Kevin Durant left the Oklahoma City Thunder to sign a contract with the Golden State Warriors.

The Warriors were already stacked with talent—they had just set an NBA record for most victories in a season. The rich got richer, and the Warriors took the notion of the superteam to a new level, easily claiming the NBA title the following season. For good or bad, the superteam was here to stay, and the roar of the fans largely drowned out the critics of this new era.

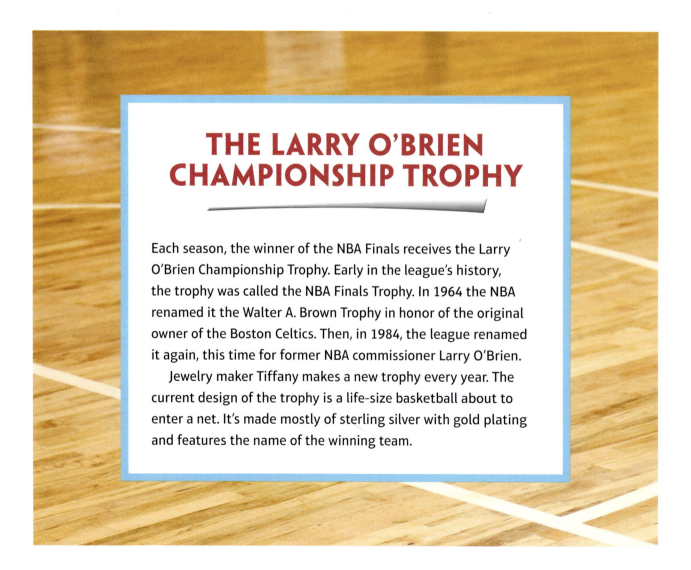

THE LARRY O'BRIEN CHAMPIONSHIP TROPHY

Each season, the winner of the NBA Finals receives the Larry O'Brien Championship Trophy. Early in the league's history, the trophy was called the NBA Finals Trophy. In 1964 the NBA renamed it the Walter A. Brown Trophy in honor of the original owner of the Boston Celtics. Then, in 1984, the league renamed it again, this time for former NBA commissioner Larry O'Brien.

Jewelry maker Tiffany makes a new trophy every year. The current design of the trophy is a life-size basketball about to enter a net. It's made mostly of sterling silver with gold plating and features the name of the winning team.

2 FROM HANNUM TO KING JAMES:
THE GREATEST GAMES OF THE NBA PLAYOFFS

Almost seven decades of the NBA playoffs have given fans loads of thrills, chills, and heartbreak. From stunning upsets to spirited comebacks to double- and triple-overtime nail-biters, the stars of the NBA have provided plenty of memorable games. Read on to learn about some of the greatest.

THE DAWN OF A DYNASTY
1957 NBA FINALS, GAME 7 • CELTICS 125, HAWKS 123

The 1957 NBA Finals marked the beginning of a heated, though short-lived, rivalry between the Celtics and the St. Louis Hawks. The two teams would go on to meet four times in the NBA Finals, and they kicked it all off in a big way. The 1957 Finals might be the greatest in NBA history, and the winner-take-all Game 7 was the jewel of the series.

It was a game of streaks. Boston surged to a 41–32 lead, but the Hawks roared back to take a two-point advantage into halftime. The Celtics took control in the third quarter, but once again, the Hawks answered with a furious rally. With less than a minute remaining in the fourth quarter, the Hawks led, 101–100. St. Louis had the ball, and Jack Coleman set up for a shot. But Bill Russell, a force on both ends of the court, swatted the shot away and then scored a basket to put Boston back in front.

The Hawks failed to score on their next possession. Desperate, they fouled Boston guard Bob Cousy. The league had no three-point line at the time, so Cousy could have put the game out of reach by making both free throws. But the dependable guard made just one, leaving the door open for the Hawks. They didn't waste the opportunity. In the closing seconds,

Bob Pettit reaches to block a shot against the Celtics in the 1957 NBA Finals. Pettit played in the All-Star Game in each of his 11 NBA seasons.

St. Louis star forward Bob Pettit drew a foul and drained both of his free throws. Overtime!

Foul trouble became a serious issue for St. Louis in overtime. Two Hawks players fouled out, leaving the team with few good options on the bench. Yet the Hawks wouldn't go away. Coleman hit a jumper near the end of the period to force the game into double overtime.

With St. Louis running out of players, little-used Alex Hannum, who also coached the team, came into the game. With only seconds to play in the second overtime period, the Celtics led by two points. The Hawks threw an inbound pass the length of the court to Hannum. In a desperate attempt to force a third overtime, Hannum threw the ball toward the backboard, hoping that Pettit could tip it in. It almost worked. Hannum's pass banged off the backboard, right to Pettit's raised hands. However, Pettit's attempt to tip the ball in came up just short. It rolled harmlessly off the rim, and the celebration was on for Boston. Game 7 of the 1957 Finals marked the beginning of the Celtics dynasty and kicked off a new era in the NBA.

A STROKE OF GENIUS
1976 NBA FINALS, GAME 5 • CELTICS 128, SUNS 126

The 1976 NBA Finals featured a contrast in styles. The Boston Celtics faced off against the Phoenix Suns, a franchise that wasn't even born until the peak of Boston's dynasty in the 1960s. The Celtics had a roster loaded with veterans, while the Suns were young and untested in the playoffs.

Both teams had won two games in the series when they put on what many call the greatest game in NBA history. It started out looking like a blowout at Boston Garden, with the Celtics jumping out to a 32–12 lead. But the Suns roared back to force overtime.

The Suns (*in blue*) kept up with the Celtics until the third overtime.

That's when the wildness really started. Late in the first overtime period, the teams were tied 101–101. With the clock running down, Boston forward Paul Silas signaled for a time-out. However, the Celtics didn't have any time-outs remaining. It should have been a technical foul. That would have given the Suns a free throw. But for some reason, the referee ignored the signal from Silas. The Suns were furious about the missed call as the game went into a second overtime.

Phoenix took a 110–109 lead with four seconds remaining on the clock. Boston quickly struck back. Guard John Havlicek streaked down the left side of the court, slashed toward the basket, and banked in a shot to give the Celtics the one-point lead. The clock showed no time remaining, and hundreds of Boston fans rushed the court in celebration.

While the court was in chaos, the game's officials were busy discussing the play. They decided that one second remained on the clock. The arena's security staff cleared the floor so the game could be finished.

Phoenix would have had to pass the ball the length of the court and score in one second. That was extremely unlikely. But while the court was being cleared of fans, Phoenix coach Paul Westphal had a stroke of genius. He had his players call a time-out, knowing that they didn't have any time-outs left. They got a technical foul, and Boston made a free throw. But the stoppage in play also allowed the Suns to pass the ball in from half-court, a much more manageable distance.

The Suns made good on Westphal's plan. The pass went to Gar Heard, who stood near the top of the key (the painted area that marks the free-throw lane). Heard quickly turned and fired a high-arcing shot that swished through the net as the buzzer sounded. Triple overtime! Little-used Boston forward Glenn McDonald took over in the third overtime, scoring six points, including a jumper in the final minute, to help give Boston a thrilling two-point victory.

"That was the most exciting basketball game I've ever seen," said NBA legend and broadcaster Rick Barry. "They just had one great play after another. . . . It was such an emotional and physical game for everybody involved."

MCHALE'S CLOTHESLINE
1984 NBA FINALS, GAME 4 • CELTICS 129, LAKERS 125

Few rivalries in sports can match the intensity of competition that existed between the Lakers and the Celtics in the 1980s. The league's two most successful franchises dominated the decade, trading championships and building a rivalry that helped

McHale clobbers Rambis. Both players later became NBA coaches.

send the NBA's popularity soaring. And no game highlighted that rivalry better than Game 4 of the 1984 NBA Finals.

The Lakers led the series two games to one and appeared to be in control of Game 4. Late in the third quarter, the Lakers, ahead by six points, were on a fast break. The ball went to Kurt Rambis, streaking down the right side of the court. Rambis headed straight for the basket, intent on extending the Lakers lead.

Boston forward Kevin McHale stepped up to challenge Rambis's shot. But McHale didn't swipe at the ball. Instead, he swung his arm toward Rambis's neck, taking down the Lakers forward with a violent clothesline tackle. Rambis slammed hard onto the floor.

It was a foul, but it was also a turning point in the game. McHale's takedown of Rambis sparked the Celtics. The Lakers wilted down the stretch in the face of Boston's aggression, including several key mistakes from LA superstar Magic Johnson, and the Celtics won in overtime.

Lakers coach Pat Riley put the blame on himself. "We were all very incensed about the takedown," he said of McHale's actions. "But I didn't do a good job of tamping down the anger and the emotion." McHale's clothesline of Rambis changed the tone of the game, and Boston went on to win the series in seven games.

A COMEBACK FOR THE AGES

1986 EASTERN CONFERENCE FIRST ROUND, GAME 1 • BULLETS 95, 76ERS 94

The 1986 playoffs were starting miserably for the Washington Bullets. The Philadelphia 76ers were running up and down the court on Washington, scoring almost at will. When Sedale Threatt of the 76ers made a free throw with 3:49 left in the fourth quarter, Philly's lead grew to a seemingly unbeatable 94–77.

Then Washington started one of the most improbable comebacks in the history of the league. While the Bullets drained

Julius Erving's athletic moves near the basket couldn't help the 76ers beat the Bullets in 1986.

shots from all over the court, the 76ers fell apart. Suddenly, they couldn't shoot. They couldn't rebound. They turned the ball over. The Bullets took advantage of almost every mistake, storming back to within a basket.

But Washington's desperate rally appeared to run out of time. In the closing seconds, the 76ers clung to a 94–92 lead. Philly legend Julius Erving was fouled. He stepped to the line for two free throws. If he made them both, the game was probably over. If he made just one free throw, Washington would have a chance to tie the game with a desperate three-point shot.

Erving missed the first free throw. Then he missed the second, and the Bullets snagged the rebound. They quickly called a time-out. The time-out allowed them to pass the ball in from half-court rather than the far end. The pass went to Dudley Bradley, who spun as defenders rushed toward him. Bradley, who had been one of the worst shooters in the NBA that season, wheeled toward the basket and heaved an off-balance shot. The ball banked off the backboard and through the net.

The comeback was complete. Over the last 3:49 of the game, the Bullets outscored the 76ers 18–0. They capped it off with a buzzer-beater that was almost more unbelievable than the comeback itself.

MILLER EXPLODES
1995 EASTERN CONFERENCE SEMIFINALS, GAME 1 • PACERS 107, KNICKS 105

Reggie Miller was one of the greatest shooters in NBA history, and his talent was never more on display than in the 1994 playoffs. His performance for the Indiana Pacers in Game 1 of the conference semifinals against the New York Knicks is one that basketball fans will never forget.

New York's Madison Square Garden was buzzing in the final minute of the game. It was the third straight year that the Knicks and Pacers had met in the playoffs, and the rivalry had reached a fever pitch. Leading the cheers from

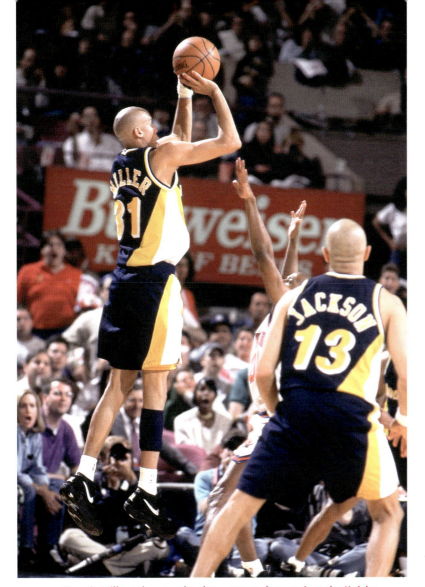

Reggie Miller takes another long-range shot against the Knicks. Miller made 2,560 three-point shots in his career, the second most in NBA history.

the first row was film director and die-hard Knicks fan Spike Lee, who had been verbally sparring with Miller all game long. Miller was more than willing to trash-talk with Lee. But in the final seconds, Miller's play would leave the director speechless.

The Knicks appeared to have the game in hand, leading 105–99 with just 18 seconds to go. That's when things got wild. Indiana's Mark Jackson fired an inbound pass to Miller, who immediately made a long three-point shot to pull within three points. New York, out of time-outs, had to inbound the ball from under their basket. The pass attempt was a disaster, and Miller stole the ball. He turned, dribbled once, and launched another three-pointer. *Swish!* Just like that, it was tied.

Indiana fouled guard John Starks on the following play. Starks stepped to the line for two free throws, but he missed them both. Knicks center Patrick Ewing tried to tap in a rebound, but the ball rolled off the rim—right into Miller's hands.

The Knicks made matters worse by immediately fouling Miller, one of the game's best free-throw shooters. He stepped to the line and calmly drained both shots. Miller had scored eight points in just nine seconds to stun the Knicks and their fans, including Spike Lee. New York was unable to take a shot on the following possession, and the Pacers walked off the court with one of the most shocking comeback wins in NBA history.

THE FLU GAME
1997 NBA FINALS, GAME 5 • BULLS 90, JAZZ 88

By 1997 Michael Jordan had become the league's biggest superstar by leading the Chicago Bulls to four NBA championships. But Game 5 of the 1997 Finals turned Jordan into a legend. The Chicago Bulls and Utah Jazz went into Game 5 of the 1997 Finals with two wins apiece in the series. It was a pivotal game that neither team wanted to lose, but the Bulls were in danger of playing without the game's greatest player. Jordan was violently ill the day of the game. A case of the flu—or possibly food poisoning—had left him feeling weak and dehydrated. The illness would have kept most players on the bench or in bed, but it was the Finals, and Jordan wasn't going to miss the game.

Fans know Game 5 of the 1997 NBA Finals as the Flu Game, but most people think Michael Jordan probably had food poisoning.

Early on, suiting up for the game looked like a questionable decision. Jordan appeared sluggish. He wasn't as dominant as usual. Utah took advantage, building a 10-point lead in the fourth quarter.

That's when Jordan took over the game. Tapping into reserves of energy that no one could have guessed he had, Jordan became a scoring machine, blowing past the Utah defense on play after play as the Bulls charged back. On the court, he looked like a man possessed. Off the court during breaks in the action, he appeared on the brink of collapse.

The game was tied 85–85 in the final minute of the fourth quarter. Jordan passed the ball to teammate Scottie Pippen. As Pippen looked for a shot, Utah's defense rushed toward him. Pippen quickly zipped the ball back out to Jordan, beyond the three-point line. Jordan rose up and launched a shot that sailed through the net. The score gave him 38 points on the night, and Chicago held on for a critical victory.

As the horn sounded to end the game, Jordan leaned on Pippen, needing help to walk off the floor. Two days later, a healthy Jordan scored 39 points to finish off the Jazz and win the NBA championship.

JORDAN DOES IT AGAIN
1998 NBA FINALS, GAME 6 • BULLS 87, JAZZ 86

A year after Jordan's epic Flu Game, the Bulls and Jazz met in a classic rematch. As good as the 1997 Finals had been, the sequel may have been even better. Jordan and the Bulls were driving for their sixth title of the decade. John Stockton, Karl Malone, and the Utah Jazz stood in their way. The series was filled with a sense of urgency on both sides. Jordan was mulling retirement, while Malone and Stockton, both in their mid-30s, knew that their championship window in Utah would soon close. Utah fans packed the Delta Center in Salt Lake City,

Utah, knowing that the Jazz needed a win to force a deciding Game 7 in the series. It had been a hard-fought and tightly contested series between the teams with that season's best regular-season records.

The game started out badly for the Bulls. All-Star Scottie Pippen threw down a dunk to score the first two points of the game, but he hurt his back on the play. Pippen gutted it out, playing 26 minutes in the game, but he was a shadow of his normal self.

The Jazz took advantage of Pippen's injury and carried a 66–61 lead into the fourth quarter. Although the Bulls didn't have Pippen at full strength, they still

When Jordan hit his game-winning shot against the Jazz, fans were already used to seeing him do incredible things on the court. Many consider him to be the greatest basketball player of all time.

had the game's greatest player in Jordan. He led the charge back, sliding through the Utah defense and draining jump shots from inside and outside.

With 20 seconds to go, the Jazz clung to a one-point lead. Utah passed the ball to Malone. Malone backed toward the basket, keeping the ball away from his defender. Malone's nickname was the Mailman because he always delivered, and this was his trademark move. Malone turned to shoot, but Jordan saw the play coming. As Malone pivoted, Jordan swatted the ball out of his hands. Malone fell to the floor as Jordan led the Bulls to the other end of the court.

The Bulls set up their offense. Jordan dribbled the ball as defender Bryon Russell shadowed him. As the clock ticked under 10 seconds, Jordan made his move. He sliced inside the three-point line and beat Russell with a crossover dribble, changing directions in a heartbeat. Russell couldn't keep up with the move—although Utah fans still insist that Jordan pushed Russell—and for a moment, Jordan was open. He rose and launched a 20-foot jumper that put the Bulls in front, 87–86.

Stunned, the Jazz tried for a miracle buzzer-beater. But Stockton's three-pointer was off the mark. Jordan and the Bulls had done it. "I never doubted myself," Jordan said. "I never doubted the whole game." His game-winning shot was his last with the Chicago Bulls, and it cemented his legacy as perhaps the greatest player in NBA history.

"ONE LUCKY SHOT DESERVES ANOTHER"
2004 WESTERN CONFERENCE SEMIFINALS, GAME 5 • LAKERS 74, SPURS 73

The Lakers, led by Kobe Bryant and Shaquille O'Neal, were building another dynasty in the 2000s. The one team in the Western Conference that consistently challenged them was the San Antonio Spurs. The two powerhouses clashed many times over that decade, but no game was more memorable than Game 5 of the Western Conference Semifinals. The Spurs won the first two games of the series

Tim Duncan shoots over Shaquille O'Neal to give San Antonio the lead with less than half a second on the game clock.

only to watch the Lakers come back to win Games 3 and 4. It set up a pivotal Game 5 in San Antonio.

It was a hard-fought, defensive struggle. Centers Tim Duncan of the Spurs and O'Neal of the Lakers clogged the middle of the court, making it difficult for anyone to score. The Lakers, on the strength of a roster that included future Hall of Famers O'Neal, Bryant, Karl Malone, and Gary Payton, slowly pulled away. Los Angeles built a lead that grew as high as 17 points before the Spurs charged all the way back in the fourth quarter.

San Antonio held a 71–70 lead as the game clock ticked under 12 seconds. Guard Kobe Bryant made a move toward the rim and then pulled up and fired a jumper. Fans in the arena let out a collective groan as the shot went through the hoop to put the Lakers back in front.

The Spurs took over. With just five seconds remaining, Manu Ginobili passed the ball to Duncan. The plan was for Duncan to pass it right back to Ginobili, who would shoot for a quick-hitting play.

But O'Neal was all over Duncan, denying him a passing lane. So Duncan improvised. He took two dribbles to the top of the key. With just two seconds remaining, he rose up, fading away to shoot over the outstretched arms of O'Neal. The crowd roared as the ball went through the hoop with just 0.4 remaining on the clock. The Spurs led, 73–72! Duncan's clutch shot left the Lakers staring in disbelief, probably wondering how they'd let such an important game slip away.

Fans might have remembered Duncan's shot as one of the greatest in playoff history if not for what came next. After a pair of time-outs, the Lakers had the ball on the side of the court. With so little time on the clock, their options were limited. The Spurs blanketed Bryant, preventing him from taking the inbound pass, so Payton passed it to solid but unspectacular guard Derek Fisher. In one fluid motion, Fisher caught the pass, turned, and chucked a quick shot toward the rim. Somehow, it went through. The Lakers sprinted off the court to celebrate. The Spurs and their fans looked on in shock at one of the most thrilling and unlikely finishes in NBA playoff history.

O'Neal, always a favorite of reporters looking for a good quote, summed it up best: "One lucky shot deserves another," he said.

BRINGING THE HEAT
2013 NBA FINALS, GAME 6 • HEAT 103, SPURS 100

The San Antonio Spurs were a model of NBA excellence throughout the 2000s and early 2010s. Center Tim Duncan wasn't the flashiest superstar in the league, but he was a winner. Entering Game 6 of the 2013 NBA Finals, Duncan and the Spurs were one win away from their fifth NBA title. All that stood in their way was the Miami Heat's LeBron James, Dwyane Wade, Chris Bosh, and others.

The Spurs appeared to be in control. Miami had no answer for Duncan near the basket, and San Antonio racked up points. By late in the third quarter, the

LeBron James takes a shot as he falls away from the basket. Playing for the Heat and the Cleveland Cavaliers, James helped his team reach the Finals every year between 2011 and 2018.

Spurs led, 71–58, and San Antonio fans could almost taste another championship.

To start the fourth quarter, San Antonio head coach Gregg Popovich left Duncan on the bench for a short rest. The Heat wasted no time taking advantage of Duncan's absence. James took over, scoring 11 points. Soon the Spurs lead had vanished, and the Miami crowd roared.

Even with Duncan back in the game, everything continued going right for Miami. During one possession, forward Mike Miller lost his shoe. He couldn't stop to put it back on, so he tossed it off the court instead. James zipped a pass to the one-shoed Miller, who calmly sank a three-pointer.

The Heat claimed an 89–86 lead with about two minutes left in the game. That's when San Antonio guard Tony Parker made his mark. Parker knocked down a long three-pointer and then dropped in a tricky layup on the following possession to put the Spurs back on top. After a James turnover and two free throws by Manu Ginobili, the San Antonio lead was 93–89. On the Heat's next possession, James launched a three-pointer that missed.

Just 28 seconds remained on the clock. San Antonio had a four-point lead and the ball, and arena officials began preparing for a Spurs celebration. The game was already a classic, but what followed would make it a game no one would ever forget.

The Heat fouled Ginobili to stop the game clock. He made one of two free throws, extending the lead to five points. Miami took over. Knowing that the Heat would probably shoot three-pointers to try to catch up quickly, the Spurs elected to take Duncan—a rebounding machine who usually played close to the basket—out of the game in favor of a better three-point shot defender.

James took a pass and threw up a quick three-point attempt. The shot missed badly, clanking off the bottom of the backboard. Three Spurs players were near the rebound, but somehow Miami guard Dwyane Wade batted the ball up and out of their reach. It trickled toward the side of the court, where Miller scooped it up. He spotted James behind the three-point line and tossed a quick pass. Before the San Antonio defense could cover James, he fired a shot. *Swish!*

The Heat quickly fouled Leonard on the following possession. He missed the first free throw and then made the second. The Spurs led 95–92.

Miami was out of time-outs, so they had to go the length of the court to score. Heat guard Mario Chalmers charged up the court with the ball. Parker was guarding James closely, but Miami's Chris Bosh got in Parker's way with a screen, leaving James open. Chalmers didn't hesitate, zipping a pass to the game's best player. Two Spurs defenders rushed toward James to contest his shot as he launched a deep three-pointer. The ball bounced off the back of the rim.

James hangs on the rim after a slam dunk. For his career, he has averaged almost 29 points per game in the playoffs.

The Spurs, still without Duncan on the court, could not secure the rebound. Bosh ended up with the ball. He zipped a pass to sharpshooting guard Ray Allen in the corner. With five seconds remaining, Allen rose up and made a three-pointer. Tie game! Parker missed a jump shot as the buzzer sounded, sending the game to overtime.

The teams traded baskets in the first several minutes of overtime. With 1:43 left on the game clock, James knocked down a jump shot that put Miami in the lead 101–100. Neither team could score over the next minute and a half. With nine seconds to go, Wade missed a jump shot and San Antonio secured the rebound. The Spurs elected not to use a time-out. Instead, Ginobili charged down the court and headed straight for the rim.

Ray Allen saw it coming. He quickly stripped the ball away as Ginobili rose up for the shot. San Antonio fouled Allen, who hit both free throws. Bosh sealed the stunning win with a block of Danny Green's desperation heave at the end, and the Miami fans went wild.

"It was by far the best game I've ever been a part of," James said. "The ups and downs, the roller coaster, the emotions, good and bad throughout the whole game."

KING JAMES BRINGS ONE HOME
2016 NBA FINALS, GAME 7 • CAVALIERS 93, WARRIORS 89

The Cleveland Cavaliers and Golden State Warriors met in the NBA Finals four straight times from 2015 to 2018. The series featured one epic clash after another, with the league's two premiere superteams butting heads. And while the Warriors won the championship in 2015, 2017, and 2018, Cleveland's LeBron James almost single-handedly denied them another title in 2016.

The Warriors took a 3–1 lead in the series, putting the Cavs on the edge of elimination. Cleveland needed to win three in a row against a team that had just

James pins the ball to the backboard in one of the greatest defensive plays in NBA playoffs history.

set an NBA record for wins by going 73–9 during the regular season. Yet James scored 41 points in each of the next two contests to force Game 7.

The thrilling game featured 11 ties and 20 lead changes. With less than two minutes to play and the score tied at 89, Cleveland's Kyrie Irving drove to the hoop, but he couldn't sink the shot. Golden State's Andre Iguodala grabbed the rebound and dribbled the ball down the court on a fast break. He threw a quick pass to the streaking Stephen Curry, who passed it right back to Iguodala for what appeared to be an easy basket. But James was rushing down the court to catch up to the ball. As Iguodala took the shot, James swatted the ball away, pinning it for a moment against the backboard.

The teams exchanged scoreless possessions, and the clock ticked under one minute with the score still tied. That's when Irving got free of a defender and drilled a three-pointer—the first points either team had scored in more than three minutes. Curry, the NBA's Most Valuable Player that season, tried to get the points back with a three-pointer of his own, but his shot was off the mark. The Warriors fouled James, who made a free throw with 10 seconds to play to put the game out of reach.

It was an amazing performance for James. He finished with 27 points, 11 rebounds, and 11 assists. His chase-down block of Iguodala's shot helped win the NBA Finals. It may have been the most important play of the game and the season.

Tears filled his eyes as he celebrated the amazing comeback with his teammates. Earlier he had promised the fans in Cleveland an NBA title. "I'm coming home with what I said I was going to do," James said. "I can't wait to get off that plane, hold that trophy up and see all our fans at the [airport]." Delivering on his promise of a title for his hometown fans remains one of the most iconic moments in NBA history.

3 FROM LEGENDS TO LAYUPS:
MEMORABLE MOMENTS OF THE NBA PLAYOFFS

Sometimes a single play, performance, or moment can make a lasting impression on fans. Miracle buzzer-beaters, seemingly impossible shots, and stunning upsets can leave fans breathless. Read on to learn about some of the moments that die-hard NBA fans will never forget.

RUSSELL'S FINEST MOMENT
1962 NBA FINALS, GAME 7 • CELTICS 110, LAKERS 107

Bill Russell was the heart of the Boston Celtics' dynasty of the 1960s. Year after year, he willed his team to victory. Russell had no shortage of memorable moments and iconic plays, but no performance stands out more than what he did in the deciding game of the 1962 NBA Finals.

Put simply, Russell, who played every minute of the hard-fought battle, was unstoppable. The center scored 30 points and snagged 40 rebounds as the Celtics edged the Lakers 110–107 in overtime. His monster game stood out amid a career filled with jaw-dropping achievements, and it helped earn him the nickname Mr. Game 7.

HAVLICEK STOLE THE BALL!
1965 EASTERN CONFERENCE FINALS, GAME 7 • CELTICS 110, 76ERS 109

The 1965 Eastern Conference Finals was a battle between the two biggest stars of the era, Bill Russell of the Celtics and Wilt Chamberlain of the 76ers. Yet the defining play of that series—and perhaps of the entire Celtics' dynasty—didn't come from either of those superstars. It came from Boston guard John Havlicek.

The Celtics were clinging to a 110–109 lead with five seconds to go in the deciding game of the series. Philadelphia's Hal Greer was set to throw an inbound pass from under his own basket. It seemed likely that the 76ers would try to get the ball to Chamberlain, whose size and strength made him all but unstoppable near the rim.

Havlicek and the Celtics played tight defense, trying to make it difficult for Greer to throw the ball inbounds. Havlicek knew that Greer had just five seconds to make the pass, so he counted off the seconds in his head. When he got to four,

Bill Russell averaged 22.5 rebounds per game during his 13-year NBA career.

FROM LEGENDS TO LAYUPS: MEMORABLE MOMENTS OF THE NBA PLAYOFFS

Havlicek (*rear*) steals the ball to secure the win for Boston.

he knew that Greer would be desperate. So for an instant, Havlicek took his eye off the man he was guarding to look back at Greer. It was good timing. At that exact moment, Greer tried tossing a high pass over Havlicek's head.

Havlicek reached out his arm and swatted the ball, deflecting it to a teammate. The Boston fans in the arena roared, while those listening on the radio heard one of the most famous calls in NBA history. "Havlicek stole the ball!" shouted an excited Johnny Most, the radio voice of the Celtics. "It's all over! It's all over. . . . Oh my, what a play by Havlicek!"

The Celtics defeated the Lakers in the NBA Finals for their seventh straight title, and Havlicek's steal remains one of the most memorable moments of their dynasty.

LONG SHOT
1970 NBA FINALS, GAME 3 • KNICKS 111, LAKERS 108

Just a few seconds remained in Game 3 of the 1970 NBA Finals after Dave DeBusschere knocked down a short jump shot to give the New York Knicks a 102–100 advantage. The Lakers had no time-outs remaining, leaving them with few options and their fans with little reason for hope.

The Lakers had three seconds to move the ball the length of the court and score. That didn't give them enough time to set up a fancy play. They had to go too far in too short a time. Luckily for the Lakers, they had guard Jerry West.

Wilt Chamberlain threw an inbound pass to West. The Lakers guard turned, dribbled twice toward half-court, and then heaved the ball toward the rim. The high-arcing shot traveled 60 feet (18 m) before miraculously dropping through the net as time ran out. In the modern NBA, it would have been a game-winning three-pointer. But the NBA had not yet adopted the three-point shot in 1970, so West's score was only good enough to tie the game and force overtime. The Lakers couldn't keep the magic going in the extra period. The Knicks went on to win the game and, eventually, the series.

Wilt Chamberlain grabs the ball in the 1970 Finals. Chamberlain was a dominant force in the NBA from 1959 to 1973.

THE LEGEND OF WILLIS REED
1970 NBA FINALS, GAME 7 • KNICKS 113, LAKERS 99

West's miracle shot in Game 3 of the 1970 Finals wasn't the only unforgettable moment in one of the league's greatest playoff series. An even bigger moment was yet to come.

Forward Willis Reed had been a wrecking ball for the New York Knicks in the series. Reed had averaged almost 32 points per game against the Lakers in the first four games, putting the Knicks on the brink of a championship. Then, in Game 5, disaster struck. Reed tore a muscle in his right thigh. It appeared that his season was over.

With Reed out of action in Game 6, the Knicks were no match for the Lakers. Wilt Chamberlain was a force of nature near the basket on both ends of the court, scoring 45 points and grabbing 27 rebounds. Without Reed, the Knicks couldn't slow down Chamberlain, and they had little reason to expect a different outcome in Game 7.

Reed was in agony from his injury and from watching his team struggle without him. "I wanted

Willis Reed (*right*) tries to see past Wilt Chamberlain during Game 7. Reed was named the 1970 Finals Most Valuable Player.

to play," Reed said. "That was for the championship, the one great moment you play for all your life. I didn't want to have to look at myself in the mirror 20 years later and say I wished I had tried to play."

So Reed did what he had to do to get onto the court. A numbing shot in his leg dulled the pain. Minutes before tip-off, Reed electrified the New York fans by limping to the court in uniform. The crowd roared as fans realized that Reed was going to play, and those cheers grew even louder as their star scored the first two baskets of the game.

Reed was nowhere near full strength. His two early baskets would be his only points of the game. But while his offense lagged, he did the job on defense that the Knicks desperately needed him to do—he slowed down Chamberlain. He gave his teammates and fans an emotional boost that helped push the Knicks over the Lakers, 113–99, to secure the franchise's first NBA title.

DR. J MAKES A LAYUP
1980 WESTERN CONFERENCE FINALS, GAME 4 • 76ERS 105, LAKERS 102

Julius Erving, known to fans as Dr. J, was a unique talent. He was a supreme athlete, famous for his gravity-defying leaping ability and his thunderous slam dunks. But his most famous shot—and one of the most celebrated shots in NBA history—wasn't a dunk at all. It was a layup.

It wasn't just any layup. The shot came in Game 4 of a heated Western Conference Finals matchup, with the 76ers and Lakers locked in a fierce, back-and-forth battle.

Midway through the fourth quarter of a tight game, Erving got the ball on the right side of the court. His defender was Mark Landsberger, a player known for his large size more than his speed or agility. It was a mismatch, and Erving knew it. He darted toward the baseline, slipping cleanly by the slower Landsberger. Erving launched himself into the air, clearly planning to throw down one of his trademark dunks.

This is how NBA fans usually saw Julius Erving score—soaring through the air before slamming the ball through the hoop.

That's when Kareem Abdul-Jabbar got in his way. The Lakers center cut off Erving's path to the basket. Already in the air, Erving adjusted, shifting his weight and swinging his arm behind the backboard. The move allowed him to squeeze past Abdul-Jabbar, but it left him in what appeared to be a hopeless position to score.

Erving's body sailed under the rim. Then he swung his arm back under the backboard and dropped the ball in from the far side of the rim. It was a layup in a league where most fans considered layups dull and ordinary. Yet Dr. J's soaring reverse score may have been the most spectacular layup in the history of the league.

Magic Johnson watched in awe. "Here I was, trying to win a championship, and my mouth just dropped open," Johnson said. "He actually did that. . . . It's still the greatest move I've ever seen in a basketball game, the all-time greatest."

Erving's amazing shot helped Philadelphia to a 105–102 victory. But the Lakers got the last laugh, winning the series on their way to another NBA title.

IT'S NO DISGUISE
1986 EASTERN CONFERENCE SEMIFINALS, GAME 2 • CELTICS 135, BULLS 131

Most basketball fans regard Michael Jordan as the greatest player in NBA history. However, in 1986, Jordan was just finishing his second season. He was one of the league's rising stars, but he was just scratching the surface of the legend he would become.

Jordan had missed 64 games—the bulk of the regular season—after suffering a broken foot. Without him, the Bulls finished the season with a dismal 30–52 record. Yet in a top-heavy Eastern Conference that had just a few great teams, that unimpressive record qualified Chicago for the eighth and final playoff spot. Jordan, back on the court for the playoffs, was set to square off with the NBA's best team, the Celtics.

Larry Bird (*center left*) tries to keep Michael Jordan away from the basket, but no one could stop Jordan in Game 2.

Even with a healthy Jordan, the Bulls were hopelessly overmatched. Chicago wouldn't win a game in the series. Yet that didn't stop Jordan from putting on a show that erased all doubt that he could become one of the game's greatest players. In Game 2 of the series, he shot and dunked his way to a stunning 63 points, an NBA playoffs record. Boston won the game in double overtime, despite Jordan's scoring explosion. Yet it was his shocking playmaking ability that had fans and players talking.

"I didn't think anyone was capable of doing what Michael has done to us," said Boston's Larry Bird after the game. "He is the most exciting, awesome player in the game today. I think it's just God disguised as Michael Jordan."

ISIAH'S BIG QUARTER
1988 NBA FINALS, GAME 6 • LAKERS 103, PISTONS 102

Dynamic guard Isiah Thomas was the heart of the powerful Detroit Pistons in the late 1980s. Thomas was tough as nails, and that was never more evident than in Game 6 of the 1988 NBA Finals.

In the third quarter, the Pistons and Lakers were engaged in a physical back-and-forth battle. Thomas was doing the offensive work for Detroit, scoring 14 straight points for his team. Then disaster struck. He badly twisted his ankle when he landed on an opponent's foot. Thomas limped to the bench in obvious pain.

He didn't stay there long. The Pistons needed Thomas, so he quickly returned to the court. Limping on his sore ankle, he picked up right where he left off, scoring from all over the floor. Cameras famously caught Thomas hopping down the court after making a layup, trying not to put any extra weight on the bad ankle.

Despite the injury, in the third quarter Thomas torched the Lakers for 25 points. His offensive surge would have been impressive anyway, but doing it while in such pain made it all the more amazing. Thomas's gutty performance left a lasting impression, but it wasn't enough. The Lakers held on for the win before claiming the championship in Game 7.

Thomas's sore ankle didn't stop him from scoring 43 points in the game.

CINDERELLA LIVES IN DENVER
1994 WESTERN CONFERENCE SEMIFINALS, GAME 5 • NUGGETS 98, SUPERSONICS 94

Hope was in short supply for the Denver Nuggets in the opening round of the 1994 Western Conference playoffs. The eight-seeded Nuggets matched up against the conference's best team, the Seattle SuperSonics, in a five-game series. No eight seed had ever won an NBA playoff series. Most fans weren't surprised when the SuperSonics blasted the Nuggets in the first two games. Seattle looked completely dominant and needed just one more victory to advance to the next round.

Denver showed life, however, winning the next two games on their home court. The series was heading back to Seattle—where the SuperSonics had a 39–4 record that year—for a deciding Game 5.

Seattle used its suffocating defense to try to force the underdog Nuggets to commit errors. But Denver was ready, relying on safe and sure-handed passes to beat the Seattle pressure. Tension in the building ran high as the game went into overtime.

In the grinding, defensive overtime session, the Nuggets clung to a two-point lead in the final minute. Seattle forward Shawn Kemp drove toward the basket.

Dikembe Mutombo blocks a shot against the SuperSonics in Game 5. Mutombo's 3,289 career blocks rank second in NBA history.

But Denver center Dikembe Mutombo swatted away Kemp's shot. Denver took control of the ball, forcing the SuperSonics to foul to stop the game clock. Robert Pack made both free throws to put Denver ahead by four points.

The SuperSonics desperately threw up a barrage of shots in the final seconds. None of them was on target. Mutombo grabbed the final rebound as the clock ticked down to zero. He clutched the ball, lying flat on the floor, as his teammates stormed the court to celebrate.

Only one other team has matched Denver's feat. In 1999 the eight-seeded New York Knicks defeated the Miami Heat. But the Nuggets did it first, and many sportswriters and fans agree that Denver's victory over Seattle in 1994 was the greatest upset in the history of the NBA playoffs.

IVERSON SHOCKS THE LAKERS
2001 NBA FINALS, GAME 1 •
76ERS 107, LAKERS 101

The 2001 Lakers appeared unstoppable. Los Angeles shredded the Western Conference, winning 11 straight playoff games on their way to the NBA Finals. The Philadelphia 76ers, meanwhile, had to scratch and claw their way through the Eastern Conference, needing a full seven games to win both the conference semifinals and conference finals.

Allen Iverson blows past Shaquille O'Neal. Iverson's quickness and agility made him one of the hardest players in the league to guard.

Lakers fans filled the arena for Game 1, expecting more dominance from their team. Instead, they witnessed one of the greatest one-man shows in the history of the NBA playoffs. Philly guard Allen Iverson was all over the court, slashing to the hoop and throwing up jump shots from every angle. At one point, Iverson executed an incredible crossover dribble that sent Lakers defender Tyronn Lue stumbling and reeling as Iverson stepped back and sank another jumper.

Iverson finished with 48 points, and the 76ers won the game in overtime. However, as impressive as Iverson was in Game 1, the 76ers were no match for Shaquille O'Neal, Kobe Bryant, and the Lakers. LA went on to win the next four games and the NBA championship.

SUPERTEAM
2017 NBA FINALS, GAME 5 • WARRIORS 129, CAVALIERS 120

What the 2017 NBA playoffs lacked in drama, they made up for in jaw-dropping history. Coming off a loss to the Cavaliers in the 2016 Finals, the Warriors added superstar Kevin Durant and then proceeded to torch the rest of the league. The Warriors rolled through the Western

Stephen Curry jumps for a layup. He won the NBA Most Valuable Player award in 2015 and 2016.

FROM LEGENDS TO LAYUPS: MEMORABLE MOMENTS OF THE NBA PLAYOFFS

Conference playoffs, sweeping Portland, Utah, and San Antonio. Then they won the first three games of the NBA Finals in a rematch against Cleveland to push their playoff winning streak to 15 games.

The Cavs managed to win Game 4, handing the Warriors their first loss of the playoffs. But it hardly mattered. Durant, Stephen Curry, and the Warriors promptly closed out the series in Game 5, 129–120. The outcome was never in doubt, and the series itself was largely forgettable. What isn't forgettable is that the Warriors went 16–1 in the playoffs, the best record in league history.

JAMES TAKES IT TO THE BANK
2018 EASTERN CONFERENCE SEMIFINALS, GAME 3 •
CAVALIERS 105, RAPTORS 103

Time was running out on the Toronto Raptors in Game 3 of the 2018 Eastern Conference Semifinals. After the top-seeded Raptors had dropped the first two games of the seven-game series at home to the Cleveland Cavaliers, it was as close to a must-win game as it could get.

The Cavs appeared ready to roll over the Raptors, building a 16-point lead late in the third quarter. But the Raptors stormed back. With just 8 seconds to go in the game, rookie OG Anunoby drained a three-point shot to pull Toronto even, 103–103.

LeBron James took the inbound pass for Cleveland. He dribbled up the left side of the court with Anunoby trying to slow him down. Near the three-point line, James used a quick crossover dribble to blast past Anunoby toward the baseline.

Less than two seconds remained as James leaped to shoot. But Anunoby had recovered and was soaring through the air, hoping to block the shot and force overtime. James improvised. He flung a high-arcing, one-handed shot toward the backboard. It was a strange-looking shot with an extreme degree of difficulty.

Fans, coaches, and players look on as James releases his last-second shot.

But the ball sailed high, bounced high off the backboard, and dropped through the net as time expired.

    Just like that, James squashed Toronto's comeback, and the legend of King James grew larger. Even his teammates struggled to explain what they'd just seen. "I ran out of words [to describe James] a while ago," said Cleveland forward Kyle Korver. "Unbelievable play. He did it again. He's been so huge in those moments for us all year."

NBA FINALS CHAMPIONS

YEAR	LEAGUE	WINNER	RUNNER-UP	SERIES	FINALS MVP*
1947	BAA	Philadelphia Warriors	Chicago Stags	4–1	—
1948	BAA	Baltimore Bullets	Philadelphia Warriors	4–2	—
1949	BAA	Minneapolis Lakers	Washington Capitols	4–2	—
1950	NBA	Minneapolis Lakers	Syracuse Nationals	4–2	—
1951	NBA	Rochester Royals	New York Knicks	4–3	—
1952	NBA	Minneapolis Lakers	New York Knicks	4–3	—
1953	NBA	Minneapolis Lakers	New York Knicks	4–1	—
1954	NBA	Minneapolis Lakers	Syracuse Nationals	4–3	—
1955	NBA	Syracuse Nationals	Fort Wayne Pistons	4–3	—
1956	NBA	Philadelphia Warriors	Fort Wayne Pistons	4–1	—
1957	NBA	Boston Celtics	St. Louis Hawks	4–3	—
1958	NBA	St. Louis Hawks	Boston Celtics	4–2	—
1959	NBA	Boston Celtics	Minneapolis Lakers	4–0	—
1960	NBA	Boston Celtics	St. Louis Hawks	4–3	—
1961	NBA	Boston Celtics	St. Louis Hawks	4–1	—
1962	NBA	Boston Celtics	Los Angeles Lakers	4–3	—
1963	NBA	Boston Celtics	Los Angeles Lakers	4–2	—
1964	NBA	Boston Celtics	San Francisco Warriors	4–1	—
1965	NBA	Boston Celtics	Los Angeles Lakers	4–1	—
1966	NBA	Boston Celtics	Los Angeles Lakers	4–3	—
1967	NBA	Philadelphia 76ers	San Francisco Warriors	4–2	—
1968	NBA	Boston Celtics	Los Angeles Lakers	4–2	—
1969	NBA	Boston Celtics	Los Angeles Lakers	4–3	Jerry West
1970	NBA	New York Knicks	Los Angeles Lakers	4–3	Willis Reed
1971	NBA	Milwaukee Bucks	Baltimore Bullets	4–0	Kareem Abdul-Jabbar
1972	NBA	Los Angeles Lakers	New York Knicks	4–1	Wilt Chamberlain
1973	NBA	New York Knicks	Los Angeles Lakers	4–1	Willis Reed
1974	NBA	Boston Celtics	Milwaukee Bucks	4–3	John Havlicek
1975	NBA	Golden State Warriors	Washington Bullets	4–0	Rick Barry
1976	NBA	Boston Celtics	Phoenix Suns	4–2	Jo Jo White
1977	NBA	Portland Trail Blazers	Philadelphia 76ers	4–2	Bill Walton
1978	NBA	Washington Bullets	Seattle SuperSonics	4–3	Wes Unseld
1979	NBA	Seattle SuperSonics	Washington Bullets	4–1	Dennis Johnson
1980	NBA	Los Angeles Lakers	Philadelphia 76ers	4–2	Magic Johnson
1981	NBA	Boston Celtics	Houston Rockets	4–2	Cedric Maxwell
1982	NBA	Los Angeles Lakers	Philadelphia 76ers	4–2	Magic Johnson

*The NBA didn't award a Finals Most Valuable Player (MVP) honor until 1969.

YEAR	LEAGUE	WINNER	RUNNER-UP	SERIES	FINALS MVP
1983	NBA	Philadelphia 76ers	Los Angeles Lakers	4–0	Moses Malone
1984	NBA	Boston Celtics	Los Angeles Lakers	4–3	Larry Bird
1985	NBA	Los Angeles Lakers	Boston Celtics	4–2	Kareem Abdul-Jabbar
1986	NBA	Boston Celtics	Houston Rockets	4–2	Larry Bird
1987	NBA	Los Angeles Lakers	Boston Celtics	4–2	Magic Johnson
1988	NBA	Los Angeles Lakers	Detroit Pistons	4–3	James Worthy
1989	NBA	Detroit Pistons	Los Angeles Lakers	4–0	Joe Dumars
1990	NBA	Detroit Pistons	Portland Trail Blazers	4–1	Isiah Thomas
1991	NBA	Chicago Bulls	Los Angeles Lakers	4–1	Michael Jordan
1992	NBA	Chicago Bulls	Portland Trail Blazers	4–2	Michael Jordan
1993	NBA	Chicago Bulls	Phoenix Suns	4–2	Michael Jordan
1994	NBA	Houston Rockets	New York Knicks	4–3	Hakeem Olajuwon
1995	NBA	Houston Rockets	Orlando Magic	4–0	Hakeem Olajuwon
1996	NBA	Chicago Bulls	Seattle SuperSonics	4–2	Michael Jordan
1997	NBA	Chicago Bulls	Utah Jazz	4–2	Michael Jordan
1998	NBA	Chicago Bulls	Utah Jazz	4–2	Michael Jordan
1999	NBA	San Antonio Spurs	New York Knicks	4–1	Tim Duncan
2000	NBA	Los Angeles Lakers	Indiana Pacers	4–2	Shaquille O'Neal
2001	NBA	Los Angeles Lakers	Philadelphia 76ers	4–1	Shaquille O'Neal
2002	NBA	Los Angeles Lakers	New Jersey Nets	4–0	Shaquille O'Neal
2003	NBA	San Antonio Spurs	New Jersey Nets	4–2	Tim Duncan
2004	NBA	Detroit Pistons	Los Angeles Lakers	4–1	Chauncey Billups
2005	NBA	San Antonio Spurs	Detroit Pistons	4–3	Tim Duncan
2006	NBA	Miami Heat	Dallas Mavericks	4–2	Dwyane Wade
2007	NBA	San Antonio Spurs	Cleveland Cavaliers	4–0	Tony Parker
2008	NBA	Boston Celtics	Los Angeles Lakers	4–2	Paul Pierce
2009	NBA	Los Angeles Lakers	Orlando Magic	4–1	Kobe Bryant
2010	NBA	Los Angeles Lakers	Boston Celtics	4–3	Kobe Bryant
2011	NBA	Dallas Mavericks	Miami Heat	4–2	Dirk Nowitzki
2012	NBA	Miami Heat	Oklahoma City Thunder	4–1	LeBron James
2013	NBA	Miami Heat	San Antonio Spurs	4–3	LeBron James
2014	NBA	San Antonio Spurs	Miami Heat	4–1	Kawhi Leonard
2015	NBA	Golden State Warriors	Cleveland Cavaliers	4–2	Andre Iguodala
2016	NBA	Cleveland Cavaliers	Golden State Warriors	4–3	LeBron James
2017	NBA	Golden State Warriors	Cleveland Cavaliers	4–1	Kevin Durant
2018	NBA	Golden State Warriors	Cleveland Cavaliers	4–0	Kevin Durant

4 LOOKING AHEAD:
THE FUTURE OF THE NBA PLAYOFFS

The NBA playoffs are bigger than ever. With massive television deals, sold-out arenas, and unforgettable rivalries, the NBA is a moneymaking machine that shows no signs of slowing down. The league's model hasn't changed much in more than three decades, but change is inevitable. What might the league look like in 10, 20, or 50 years?

PLAYOFF RESTRUCTURING

For more than three decades, the NBA's playoff formula has remained mostly constant, with 16 teams—eight from each conference—advancing to the playoffs. Meanwhile, the nonplayoff teams enter into the NBA Draft Lottery. The team with the worst record has the best chance of getting the top overall pick in the next NBA Draft.

Fans love to celebrate with their basketball heroes, and winning in the playoffs is the ultimate NBA celebration.

This method gives bad teams a better chance to improve. But the unintended consequence is tanking. In the NBA more than in any other major sport, the addition of one superstar player can vault a team into title contention. So teams that find themselves unable to compete for a championship have a strong incentive to lose and find that superstar at the top of the draft.

League officials know that tanking is bad for the game. Fans don't want to pay to watch their favorite teams lose on purpose. So the NBA has been investigating ways to prevent it. One idea is to give nonplayoff teams a chance to receive the top pick. That would reduce the incentive to lose, but it would also make it more difficult for the league's worst teams to improve. That could result in a more top-heavy league that already suffers from a gaping divide between the haves and the have-nots.

With players engineering their own superteams, changing the most effective way for bad teams to get better by tinkering with the draft could leave some franchises stuck at the bottom for years or even decades.

Some have suggested a play-in bracket, based on college basketball tournaments. Then the league's bottom teams would have a chance to play their way into an expanded playoff bracket. Having even a small chance to qualify for the playoffs could be enough to give teams the incentive to stop tanking.

Some fans feel that the playoff conference system might be outdated. In recent years, teams in the Western Conference have had better records than teams in the Eastern Conference. Yet since each conference sends eight teams to the playoffs, good teams from one conference may be left out, while bad teams from the other conference get in. Even worse, the NBA sometimes faces a Finals matchup that doesn't feature the league's two best teams—they often play each other in the conference finals instead. Some people have suggested that the NBA should choose to do away entirely with the conference system, instead, seeding the teams with the best records regardless of conference.

NBA GLOBALIZATION

In 1993 the league expanded to Canada by adding the Toronto Raptors, but every other NBA franchise is in a US city. That could soon change.

The international popularity of the NBA has exploded in recent decades. Part of the reason is an increase in foreign-born players. In the 1980–1981 season, only 1.7 percent of NBA players were born outside of the United States. By 2014–2015, that number had soared to 28.6 percent. In 2017–2018, the NBA featured 108 international players from 42 countries and territories. It's not surprising that fans around the world have a heightened interest in the league.

The NBA has responded by playing games and putting on exhibitions in countries such as Mexico, China, and the Dominican Republic. In 2014 the league unveiled NBA Global Games, a series that sent NBA teams to Brazil, the United Kingdom, and the Philippines for preseason matches. NBA commissioner Adam Silver has even suggested that overseas regular-season games may soon be added.

The NBA is driven by revenue, and there's money to be made overseas. How long will it be before the NBA starts a franchise in Mexico, the United Kingdom, or Spain? Instead of the Western Conference and the Eastern Conference, will the league have American, European, and Pacific Conferences?

According to Silver, the league has no immediate plans to expand outside of North America. Scheduling and travel would be a problem, and maintaining player security could be difficult in some places. Yet maybe someday, an NBA team based in Europe, Mexico, or China could win the Larry O'Brien Championship Trophy.

Rising stars such as Giannis Antetokounmpo (*right*), who is from Greece, have boosted the NBA's popularity around the world.

LOOKING AHEAD: THE FUTURE OF THE NBA PLAYOFFS   59

SOURCE NOTES

7 "Top Moments: Howie Dallmar, Philadelphia Warriors Win First NBA Title," NBA, accessed May 15, 2018, http://www.nba.com/history/top-moments/1947-warriors-first-title#/.

23 "Triple-OT Classic Highlights Boston's 13th Title," NBA, accessed May 21, 2018, http://www.nba.com/history/finals/19751976.html.

25 Bob Ryan, "First Contact," NBA, June 6, 2014, http://www.nba.com/hoop/1984_nba_finals__2014_06_03.html.

31 Ric Bucher, "Jordan Gets 45, Bulls Take Six," *Washington Post*, June 15, 1998, http://www.washingtonpost.com/wp-srv/sports/nba/longterm/1998/finals/articles/nba15.htm.

33 Chris Broussard, "The Spurs Win . . . No, Wait, the Lakers Win," *New York Times*, May 14, 2004, https://www.nytimes.com/2004/05/14/sports/pro-basketball-the-spurs-win-no-wait-the-lakers-win.html.

37 Paul Flannery, "NBA Finals 2013: The Inspiring, Agonizing, Amazing Story of Game 6," SB Nation, June 19, 2013, https://www.sbnation.com/nba/2013/6/19/4444298/heat-vs-spurs-nba-finals-2013-game-6-ray-allen-lebron-james.

38 "20,000 Fans Greet NBA Champion Cavaliers at Airport," UPI, June 20, 2016, https://www.upi.com/20000-fans-greet-NBA-champion-Cavaliers-at-airport/2041466452095.

42 Ian Thomsen, "After 50 Years, Havlicek's Stolen Moment Etched for Ages," NBA, April 15, 2015, http://www.nba.com/2015/news/features/ian_thomsen/04/15/havliceks-epic-stolen-moment-continues-to-live-on/.

44–45 "Reed's Game vs. Lakers Tops List," *ESPN*, May 7, 2010, http://www.espn.com/los-angeles/nba/news/story?id=5170973.

46 "Top Moments: Julius Erving Shocks Lakers with Improbable Move," NBA, accessed May 20, 2018, http://www.nba.com/history/top-moments/1980-julius-erving-lakers-76ers.

47 "God Disguised as Michael Jordan," NBA, accessed May 31, 2018, http://www.nba.com/history/jordan63_moments.html.

53 Associated Press, "He the North: LeBron's Bank at Buzzer Downs Raptors," *ESPN*, May 6, 2018, http://www.espn.com/nba/recap?gameId=401031715.

GLOSSARY

barnstorming: traveling and making brief stops to perform

baseline: the out-of-bounds line running along each end of a basketball court

buzzer-beater: a last-second basket that wins or ties the game

commissioner: the executive in charge of running a league

crossover dribble: a play in which a ball handler quickly dribbles the ball across his body and changes direction

draft: an event in which NBA teams select new players

dynasty: a period of dominance by one team that lasts several seasons

fast break: a play in which a team quickly moves the ball up the court toward the basket

franchise: a team and the organization around it, including the owner, ticket sellers, and others

inbound pass: a pass made from out of bounds to restart play

jump shot: a shot taken away from the basket in which the player's feet leave the court; also called a jumper

revenue: money earned by a business

screen: a play in which an offensive player gets in the way of a defender, helping to free a teammate for an open shot

seeded: ranked

superteam: a team of star players who chose to play together

tank: to lose games on purpose to improve a team's odds in the NBA Draft Lottery

upset: when the underdog wins a game

FURTHER READING

Books

Bryant, Howard. *Legends: The Best Players, Games, and Teams in Basketball*. New York: Philomel Books, 2017.

Doeden, Matt. *Coming Up Clutch: The Greatest Upsets, Comebacks, and Finishes in Sports History*. Minneapolis: Millbrook Press, 2019.

———. *Final Four: The Pursuit of Basketball Glory*. Minneapolis: Millbrook Press, 2016.

Savage, Jeff. *Basketball Super Stats*. Minneapolis: Lerner Publications, 2018.

Whiting, Jim. *The Story of the Boston Celtics*. Mankato, MN: Creative Education, 2015.

Websites

Basketball Reference
https://www.basketball-reference.com

ESPN.com: NBA
http://www.espn.com/nba

NBA.com
http://www.nba.com/

WNBA.com
http://www.wnba.com

YouTube: The NBA
https://www.youtube.com/user/NBA

INDEX

American Basketball Association (ABA), 13

Basketball Association of America (BAA), 7–9, 12, 54
Bird, Larry, 15, 47, 55
Black Fives, 12
Boston Celtics, 10–11, 13, 15, 18–24, 40–42, 46–47, 54–55
Bryant, Kobe, 15, 31–33, 51, 55

Chamberlain, Wilt, 41, 43–45, 54
Chicago Bulls, 15, 28–31, 46–47, 55
China, 59
Cleveland Cavaliers, 17, 37–39, 52–53, 55
Cousy, Bob, 20
Curry, Stephen, 38, 52

Dallmar, Howie, 7–8
Denver Nuggets, 13, 49–50
Detroit Pistons, 48, 55
Dominican Republic, 59
Duncan, Tim, 32–35, 37, 55
Durant, Kevin, 17, 51–52, 55
dynasty, 10–11, 15, 21, 31, 40–42

Erving, Julius "Dr. J," 26, 45–46

Golden State Warriors, 8, 17–18, 37–38, 51–52, 54–55

Havlicek, John, 22, 41–42, 54

Iguodala, Andre, 38–39, 55
Indiana Pacers, 13, 26–28, 55
Iverson, Allen, 51

James, LeBron, 17, 33–35, 37–39, 52–53, 55
Johnson, Magic, 15, 24, 46, 54–55
Jordan, Michael, 15, 28–29, 31, 46–47, 55

Larry O'Brien Championship Trophy, 18, 59
Lee, Spike, 27–28
Los Angeles Lakers, 11, 15, 23–25, 31–33, 41–46, 48, 50–51, 54–55
Lue, Tyronn, 51

Malone, Karl, 29, 31–32
McHale, Kevin, 24–25
Mexico, 59
Miami Heat, 17, 33–35, 37, 50, 55
Mikan, George, 9–10, 13
Miller, Reggie, 26–28
Minneapolis Lakers, 9–11, 54
Mutombo, Dikembe, 50

National Basketball League (NBL), 8–9, 12
NBA Draft, 56–58
NBA Draft Lottery, 56
New York Knicks, 26–28, 43–45, 50, 54–55

O'Neal, Shaquille, 15, 31–33, 51, 55

Payton, Gary, 32–33
Pettit, Bob, 21
Philadelphia 76ers, 25–26, 41, 45, 50–51, 54–55
Phoenix Suns, 21–23, 54–55
Pippen, Scottie, 29–30

Rambis, Kurt, 24–25
Reed, Willis, 44–45, 54
Russell, Bill, 13, 20, 40–41

San Antonio Spurs, 13, 31–35, 37, 52, 55
Seattle SuperSonics, 49–50, 54–55
Silver, Adam, 59
St. Louis Hawks, 19–21, 54
Stockton, John, 29, 31
superteams, 17–18, 37, 58

Thomas, Isiah, 48, 55

United Kingdom, 59
Utah Jazz, 28–31, 52, 55

Wade, Dwyane, 17, 33, 35, 37, 55
Washington Bullets, 25–26, 54
West, Jerry, 43–44, 54
Women's National Basketball Association (WNBA), 16

ABOUT THE AUTHOR

Matt Doeden began his career as a sportswriter, covering everything from high school sports to the NFL. Since then he has written hundreds of children's and young adult books on topics ranging from history to sports to current events. His book *Darkness Everywhere: The Assassination of Mohandas Gandhi* was listed among the Best Children's Books of the Year by the Children's Book Committee at Bank Street College. Doeden lives in Minnesota with his wife and two children.

PHOTO ACKNOWLEDGMENTS

Image credits: Gregory Shamus/Getty Images, pp. 4, 53, 57; Bettmann/Getty Images, pp. 6, 11; Charles T. Higgins/NBAE/Getty Images, p. 8; Bill Meurer/NY Daily News/Getty Images, p. 9; Science History Images/Alamy Stock Photo, p. 12; Focus on Sport/Getty Images, pp. 14, 41, 46; Vince Bucci/AFP/Getty Images, p. 15; Hannah Foslien/Getty Images, p. 16; Rich Schultz/Getty Images, p. 17; Richard Meek/Sports Illustrated/Getty Images, p. 20; Dick Raphael/Sports Illustrated/Getty Images, p. 22; Peter Read Miller/Sports Illustrated/Getty Images, p. 24; Jerry Wachter/Sports Illustrated/Getty Images, p. 25; Manny Millan/Sports Illustrated/Getty Images, p. 27; JEFF HAYNES/AFP/Getty Images, pp. 28, 30, 50; Wally Skalij/Los Angeles Times/Getty Images, p. 32; Hector Gabino/El Nuevo Herald/Getty Images, p. 34; Charles Trainor Jr./Miami Herald/Getty Images, p. 36; BECK DIEFENBACH/AFP/Getty Images, p. 38; Walter Iooss Jr./Sports Illustrated/Getty Images, p. 42; Dan Farrell/NY Daily News Archive/Getty Images, pp. 43, 44; Dick Raphael/NBAE/Getty Images, p. 47; Andrew D. Bernstein/NBAE/Getty Images, pp. 48, 49; Kyle Terada/Pool/Getty Images, p. 51; Stacy Revere/Getty Images, p. 59. Design elements: FabrikaSimf/Shutterstock.com, p. 1 (basketball); Billion Photos/Shutterstock.com, p. 12 (basketball court).

Front cover: Gregory Shamus/Getty Images. Flap: JEFF HAYNES/AFP/Getty Images.